I0168242

P
H
E
N
O
M
E
N
A

PHENOMENA

Lawrence Gregory

SHANTI ARTS PUBLISHING
BRUNSWICK, MAINE

Phenomena

Copyright © 2023 Lawrence Gregory

All Rights Reserved
No part of this document may be reproduced
or transmitted in any form or by any
means without prior written permission
of the publisher, except in the case of brief
quotations embodied in critical reviews.

Published by Shanti Arts Publishing

Designed by Shanti Arts Designs

Cover image is used with permission from
the artist: Patricia Pollard, *After the Rain*

Shanti Arts LLC
193 Hillside Road
Brunswick, Maine 04011
shantiarts.com

Printed in the United States of America

ISBN: 978-1-956056-80-8 (softcover)

Library of Congress Control Number: 2023932562

for Birgit

Since everything is but an apparition
Having nothing to do with good or bad
Acceptance or rejection
One may well burst out laughing

—Longchenpa (1308–1364)

Contents

THESE DAYS

AN INDULGENT SIP OF CLARITY

Acknowledgments

My heartfelt appreciation to my son, Gregory Block, and to Linda Collison, Patrina Corsetti, Birgit Gutsche, and Kim Wiltshire for their willingness to read and provide thoughtful suggestions and commentary on the original manuscript. Their discerning eyes, sharp intellects, and compassionate hearts have been invaluable.

To Christine Cote and Shanti Arts Publishing, thank you for believing in the work and bringing this collection to life.

To Pat Pollard, whose painting, "After The Rain," graces the cover of this book, I offer my sincere thanks for providing inspiration through her art and fearlessness.

I am grateful to the editors of *Crosswinds Poetry Journal* who saw fit to publish "Ethereal" in their inaugural, Fall 2021 edition.

Two poems in this collection have appeared in *Still Point Arts Quarterly*—"Streetwise, NYC" in the Spring 2021 edition and "First Light" in the Spring 2023 edition.

"After The Rain," an ekphrastic poem, was written in response to Pat Pollard's gorgeous painting of the same name. Thanks to both the Taos Center for the Arts and SOMOS (Society of the Muse of the Southwest) for collaborating on this Ekphrastic Poetry project held during April 2019 in honor of National Poetry Month.

To the members of the Kimberley Writers Group (Kimberley, British Columbia, Canada) for their critical listening to early drafts of several of the poems appearing here. And especially to Lori Craig and Kim Wiltshire for their support and encouragement.

With the exception of "So little traffic . . . " and "Deep in the canyon . . . ", the haiku in the section titled "A Momentary Pandemic" were written in response to visual artist Gregory Block's call to family, friends, and collectors to submit a haiku each day of April 2020 in recognition both of National Poetry Month and the emotional turmoil experienced by all during the early months of the COVID-19 pandemic. He published the haiku, submitted by writers from across North America, on his website: www.gregoryfblock. com. "Like a meteor . . . " and "Your arm laced through mine . . . " also first appeared in that project.

And, finally, to Birgit Gutsche—my friend and lover and wife—I hereby proclaim my ongoing amazement and gratitude for your patience and understanding through it all.

POEMS

and other high-wire acts

PHENOMENA

Like a meteor
We live this singular life
A flash of brilliance

First Light

As if
the early
morning sun
silvering the wings
        of those Sandhill cranes
circling high above
the river mist is
not enough to
satisfy—

Ethereal

Like the way you were floating
Through those last days of summer
When worn out from the road I arrived
In need of a bed, not a nickel to my name.
You offered refuge, taught me how to
Surrender in your house made of glass,
Where on the bamboo floor we held our
Postures, then held our silence looking out to sea—

Like the way the sunlight sifted through
The redwoods, trees so tall I could not tilt
My head back far enough to see their highest
Reaching, so had to lay my body down flat out
Between the lichened stones arranged just so
On the spiraled sand. In the stillness of your
Manicured Zen garden there was a fountain and
A bell somewhere sounding on the breeze—

Like the way we have always been floating,
Content to abide the inexorable ebb tide.
And now with the years heaped upon years
Like sea wrack abandoned on the shore,
I like to think of you still living alone
In Humboldt County, walking barefoot in your garden,
The late afternoon sun raking through the tall trees
Lighting you up in that faded cotton dress—

Phenomena

In the meditation hall you sit
On the cushion reciting the Heart Sutra:
Form is emptiness, emptiness is form.
On the timbered ridge a lightning flash sparks
A languid curl of blue smoke from the duff,
Aspen trees suddenly bend in the wind
While in the meadow below a woman
Dippers cool water from a bubbling spring.

In a distant hospital your mother
Lies tethered to an artificial life
And you recall words from García Márquez:
No medicine cures what happiness cannot.
The monitor monitors; the pump pumps
But ultimately every heart flatlines.

Outside the Snow Is Falling

Outside the snow is falling
and I have forgotten what to say.

But even if I could remember
the words that sometimes bring you back

you could not hear me now
over the din of childhood on the run.

Sirens and laughter weave
through a distant labyrinth of towers

and you are dreaming
in their midst, trying to stop the rain.

Outside the snow keeps falling
and though your head is resting

between my heart and yesterday,
the night is growing colder

and I am desperate to remember
the smell of freshly turned earth

resting sun-warmed and black
under the summer sky.

Tessellations

Watch
lightning spider the blue-
black sky—

Notice
how sunlight severs
the storm from its mooring

along the mesa—
the ignition of sky flares,
tessellations

of light scattering
through cottonwood
and red willow—

Listen
to rainwater river
through the arroyo,

the meadowlark sing
from its perch on
a glistening wire—

Wait
for the darkness and a crescent
moon dancing the ridgeline—

Feel
for the first time in years
you are home.

Whisper

When I was a boy, I dreamed
rings around the sun
and moon—like Saturn,

drifted through the whisper
of brittle leaves under
a cerulean sky,

while somewhere
in the blonding grass
a cricket's staccato longing.

Now,
sometimes in the night
I can sense Time

whistle and weave
through the cold, hard stars,
leaving redemption in its cosmic wake.

Your arm laced through mine
The silence awash with stars
We walk with Venus

A MOMENTARY
PANDEMIC

No choice but to stay
On the wings of April wind
Solitude arrives

What anxiety?
Even as this sunset fades
There are meadowlarks

So little traffic
Scientists can hear the earth
Solid ground adrift

In your fevered sleep
I wonder if you can feel
My hand holding yours

Who doesn't wake up
In the middle of the night
Checking for symptoms?

I write some poems
Read thought-provoking essays
But I need your touch

Truth may yet prevail
The emperor has no mask
Myths unraveling

When can we relax?
Even Basho broke the rules
Difficult, the how

One by one by one
Mark the hours, the days, the weeks
One by one by one

You say it's Sunday
I make another coffee
It could be Tuesday

Beneath a salt rim
Tequila, Triple Sec, lime
Things are better now

I yearn to hold you
Walk by your side through the fields
Drink from the same cup

Navajo Nation
Devastation descending
Staggering, the loss

Twenty creek crossings
Wind rush through the ancient trees
A fortunate path

Deep in the canyon
We watch an otter sunning
On smooth river rock

In another world
We come upon petroglyphs
Who wrote these stories?

There is no reset
The earth will keep on spinning
As it always has

Let's enjoy the ride
The universe doesn't care
It simply expands

A FIRE IN THE FEET

Fall Line

Despair travels
the teardrop's
fall line

in the illusive
search for fixity's
critical angle.

Better to repose
with Sisyphus
when Orpheus sings.

With Your Pledge,
NPR Is Offering an Attractive Tote . . .

but you wonder
if it's large enough
to hold this compromise,

this bloodless surrender
to the 19th Avenue traffic
and panic of ordinary existence.

You wander the streets—
the neither here nor there—
stumble through the anywhere

in franchised America.

Oh, exalted mediocrity!
Oh! This juddering soul.

You've become a drifter adrift
through the halogen nights,
the steel-gray mornings

melting into white.
It's dizzying,
the relentless

flat light vertigo.

A Fire in the Feet

To remain is to be complicit.

Eventually, you long
to dream again in color,

sing something other than
the fearful tribal songs.

Finally, the need
to be anywhere other

sparks a fire in the feet.

Neruda's Ghost

I must return to the land
I must return home

I must go alone

Home to that wild and forgiving place
I must leave you here today

I must go alone

To be battered by the wind
And scorched by the sun

Silenced by thunder
And chilled to the core

I am returning to my home
Where one day you will come to me

But for now, I must go alone.

Road Trip

A sunset flares over the indigo mesa and a desire to
        swallow the wind.
How far into the velvet distance before you finally
        disappear?
What color are your dreams?
The priest said, *If you don't know where you are going
        you will probably end up somewhere else.*

How far into the velvet distance before you finally
        disappear?
Wearing jeans and old T-shirts, Hope & Fear stand on
        the corner, thumbs out, waiting for a ride.
The priest said, *If you don't know where you are going
        you will probably end up somewhere else.*
Taking the alternate route lets you detour
        around the familiar insanity.

Wearing jeans and old T-shirts, Hope & Fear stand on
the corner, thumbs out, waiting for a ride.
It's easier to keep your balance when you accelerate
through the nostalgia.
Taking the alternate route lets you detour around the
familiar insanity.
Would you have made the same choices if you'd felt the
earth spinning on its tilted axis?

It's easier to keep your balance when you accelerate
through the nostalgia.
The real danger begins the moment you believe you have
reached your destination.
A sunset flares over the indigo mesa and a desire to
swallow the wind.
What color are your dreams?

Heading South

Heading south
headlong through the darkness.

Time to shake the killing frost
from these bones,

Dance a little
in the light,

Celebrate
this self-inflicted homelessness.

Dawn

Meadowlarks—
dozens of them
chant their morning mantras.

Wild horses' silver
nickering breath
steam curls

and drifts
across the hesitant
April greening steppe.

Renewal finds a way
even in this rough-
hewn country.

Escalante Dharma

Uplifted rock.
Red and black
and ochre bands

fold and twist
and eddy back
against the flow

of crystallized time
streaming through
the stillness.

•

These silent stones
are the stuff of my bones

and my blood.

This desert wind
is my breath.

On outstretched wings
the raven soars.

In America . . .

there are 333 million people
living in 131 million households,
120 million of which have at least one

refrigerator cycling on and off
and on again— every day.

But you are camped
on the rim of a nameless canyon
somewhere in southern Utah.

You walk naked across
the slickrock, alone in the silence,
showered by starlight.

Soon you will stand
With outstretched arms
To greet the rising sun.

You
Become
The light—

On the Henry's Fork

I step
into the familiar lifeblood

wade
knee-deep in river shimmer

cast deception
in graceful arcs of gossamer

to silver flash
and shadow dance.

Feeling
the tug of current

the lift of sky

I stand
poised between

two sides
of the same yearning.

Equally enticing
they beckon

in the lightning-
riven twilight.

•

Out of
the still dazzling

upriver
distance

pelicans
and cormorants

skim
the glitter and glare

spectral voices
and apparitions

everywhere
ride the careening

quicksilver current's
tumble through the canyon

and the evening's
longing coming on—

is that your voice
hitched to the wind?

Incendiary

It is impossible to know simultaneously the exact position and velocity of a particle.

—Heisenberg's Uncertainty Principle

When you carve down
to the quantum core of it
existence is a matter of probability,
an engagement with uncertainty.

From this vantage
everything appears
a fleeting revelation,
a crystalline perception flashing.

●

A rend in the earth
beckons. The jealous river—
cutter of stone, revealer
of secrets— hews the ancient
defile deeper into yesterday

while in the aftermath of last night's
thunderstorm, the morning redolent
with ozone, sage and magic,
you twist the throttle open.

On two wheels at a hundred miles an hour
asphalt unspooling inches beneath your feet,
you wonder if hurtling through the sunrise
will take you to a place worth
getting to— it's harder than you think
to leave this land where lightning
sets the world on fire.

Drafting the momentary
slipstream of awareness,
direction loses meaning
in the focus and flow.

It's a romance with adrenaline—
licking the speed of it.

Not merely to observe, but
To merge with the landscape
Is all that's ever mattered—
The courage to embrace the light,

Revel in its cascading colors,
Feeling the heat—

THESE DAYS

The myths are unraveling—

Imagine no God
Imagine no internet
Which frightens you more?

Streetwise, NYC (a found poem)

W
E
L
C
O
M
E
to all
the possibilities
the morning can
bring **HOPE** to all
violators I should
probably get a ride home
but I have already broken
free of landscapes having
nothing whatever to do with
outer reality hieroglyphic forms
glimpsed in the intimacy of their
home the eye in the picture is
buzzed staring at me driving in a
live immersive adventure I have so
many things inside of me just burst
-ing a sense of alienation a sense of
vulnerability a sense of danger **STOP**
don't be afraid of anyone make no distinction
between painting and poetry read all the news

that's fit to print don't yield to fake news fake

President making America hate again one vehicle

at a time he'll make you see in a whole new way

Wait! Really? If you see something say what you see

RESIST sitting no standing no loitering dump business

trash here watch your step exercise caution at 725 5th avenue

merge right yield to all pedestrians worshiping the sacred

what are you waiting for? Her loins are hot restricted access

authorized personnel only get willing get able get serious

imagine hard hats covering everyone smoking in New York

no piggybacking don't walk consider idling in old school zone

all philosophy classes begin all visitors must stop here on red

all Queens must check in at field office she loved New York

one way or another look special look up look down look out look left look

right   look   both   ways   make   yourself   look   unforgettable

bring your vision to life STAY TRUE but get your brand recognized

I'm free free as the guy break-dancing in Times Square time out

time's up to you What would you like the power to do? Imagine it

imagine a better future not just sparkling dazzling this location permanently closed

Wait! Really? I'm still here! Think color think coffee too many humans not enuf souls

anonymously reporting unsafe conditions I want to crush you in my arms cover you

with a million kisses give me one more chance no way shaft way Broadway be mindful

walk honestly actually literally ride free dismount dive into the black hole Zap! Stare into

the blue reach for the sun leap up stand with a friend and smile eat drink dance! Pleasure

should be fair game did they just? Would you just use me on the next available table?

Thank you for visiting we'll miss you don't worry one way or another you can keep shopping.

Who isn't engaged in the daily quest
for truth, a measure of forgiveness
and a decent night's fuck?

These Days

The young man
working the till asks
if you'd like your $2.59
in loyalty points applied to
this purchase.

You say, *Yes, please,*
Life is uncertain.

He laughs, says,
these days it is.

You smile, slide
your credit card back
in your wallet and say,
not just these days—

Recipe for Our Time

In a rusting melting pot—

Combine your hashtag heroes and social media influencers with coarse salt, righteous indignation and previously frozen reason

Fold in the treasonable senators (with donors still attached)

Gently add politically correct academics and self-important virtue signalers

Fuck the system to a boil

Reduce heat, simmer until a smooth, trivial philosophy is obtained

Remove spines—if any

Set aside to assemble in a separate, trigger-free reality

Puree the remaining deceitful assertions

Let stand until tyranny thickens and science is denied

When fear rises to desired consistency
punch down with a viral fist
Knead vigorously until the days become elastic and the
mind achieves a velvety texture

Before capitulating to mediocrity, divide conspiracy
theories equally

Garnish with astonishment

Serve chilled

In the Shoes of Another

If you haven't experienced hunger
it is impossible to understand
the desperation—

If you haven't experienced hunger
it is impossible to appreciate
your abundance—

Sonnet for Climate Change

As I eat breakfast and scan the day's news,
an iceberg twice the size of Manhattan
cleaves from a glacier in Antarctica.
Later tonight, I'll lie awake thinking
about the farcical nature of it—
the way we measure and model the speed
and degree of our feverish demise
but fail to act in significant ways.
There is irony everywhere you look.
Like the Hollywood glitteratti who
congratulate themselves for the plant-based
banquet they devour before dancing
in a hall festooned with flowers flown in
by jet from Italy and Ecuador.

AN INDULGENT
SIP OF CLARITY

Genesis

Day 1

Abandoned earth hero
Destiny under interrogation
Inquires within the womb

Appealing to the multitude
Aspiring to hagiography
A dangerous journey all the way around

Refugee or poet?
Either way a seeker
Of rhymes and reasonable expectations

Of love
Borrowed or plundered
Certain to be exchanged

For a rusty taste of experience
The bloodlust
Drips and braids

•

Peyote or mushroom
A dose of smooth magic
An exultant condensation

Our dauntless earth hero drinks:
An indulgent sip of clarity?
A bracing draft of confusion?

Either way a curious journey
around the melting rim of the world

Day 2

An instant ago
A momentary snow
Our anxious earth hero hesitates

Darker and darker
The shadows lengthen and linger
A scattering of ashes

A shudder
A cry
A glorious becoming!

Edited memory
Altered perception
Either way a lavender breeze

Caressing a violet sea
A diamond desert
A bouquet of exquisite skeletons

Storm clouds and shape shifters
Dance to a triumphant
Aquamarine music

Enter a magnificent vermillion cat
Turning cartwheels
Not what he expected

Day 3

Our intrepid earth hero
Guardian of the night
Keeper of the innermost resistance

Listens—

Bone chilling poems
Healing secrets
A symphony of compassionate refrains

Considers—

A violent destiny
A public release
A private death

Not what he expected
But, still—
Butterflies breathing life

Bringing us together
Out of the shadowlands
Together we emerge

From a blaze of white lilies
Superbly naked
Erotic hearts beating

You and I belong
Not what we expected

Day 4

Tangled reflections
Cleave the half-melted light
Music of the spheres

Speed the narrow black
Our cosmic hero
Recites a space poetry

While hurtling through
Every twisted thing
Asteroid or tramp?

Either way a wrangler
of magical moments

•

And, still— butterflies
Breathing life
Unwinding the bloodlust

Drips and braids
A sip of clarity
A private death

A riverbed cut through
The diamond desert
Fragments of bone

A scattering of ashes
Hover in the magnetic breeze
Erotic hearts beating

Day 5

Tourmaline
Turquoise
A blaze of forgotten lilies

(Glorious the altered perception!)

Invert time
Dance through the dangerous
Coincidence

Intimate spies
A grateful priestess
Desperate mothers

Explore every twisted thing
A dangerous journey beyond
A smooth magic within

●

A cry
A cringe
A shudder

A ~~violet~~ violent sea
And everywhere the earth
Is yearning

A spill of feathers
An ooze of fur
The bloodlust

The shadows lengthen and linger
A scattering of ashes
Fragments of bone

Not what anyone expected

Day 6

A starlight imagination ignites
A blaze of flamboyant lilies
Our glorious hero emerges

Victorious!

Practicing crazy
Answering outrageous
Permission to risk everything

The power to free each other
Either way a longing to embrace
A different death tomorrow

A sip of clarity
A smooth magic within
A destiny no longer in question

The blood
The lust
Superbly naked

You and I belong

The ~~power~~ desire to free each other

After the Rain

From a not quite sleep
In the not quite morning
I woke not quite ready
To relinquish the night
To the crimson confusion
The fractured light

But after the rain
In the petrichor silence
There's a new day unfolding
Washed clean of the violence
That too long has held sway

There's an easy wind rising
And fading away
An easy wind rising
And fading away

We all have the chance
To experience this life
At the speed of love

Then Again

I might better serve
the readers of my poetry

by stripping away
first one word,

then another.
A line.

Entire stanzas could
be erased

until all that remains
is the silence

of the blank page
where once again

anything is possible.

About the Author

photo: Birgit Gutsche

Lawrence Gregory's poems have appeared in literary reviews, journals, and other publications. His 2017 collection, *Stretching Silver Through Blue Haze*, a collaboration with his wife, the award-winning photographer Birgit Gutsche, was published by Shanti Arts (2017; Brunswick, Maine). They live in the rarefied air and revelatory light of northern New Mexico.

SHANTI ARTS

NATURE ▪ ART ▪ SPIRIT

Please visit us online
to browse our entire book catalog,
including poetry collections and fiction,
books on travel, nature, healing, art,
photography, and more.

Also take a look at our highly regarded art
and literary journal, *Still Point Arts Quarterly*,
which may be downloaded for free.

www.shantiarts.com

www.ingramcontent.com/pod-product-compliance
Lightning Source LLC
Chambersburg PA
CBHW050823090426
42738CB00020B/3468